Simple printmaking
Sarah Roberts

Published by Morse-Brown Publishing
Series Editor: John Morse-Brown
Photography © Morse-Brown Design Limited
Design & Production: Morse-Brown Design Limited.
↗ www.morsebrowndesign.co.uk
For more titles in this series, see ↗ www.how2crafts.com

ISBN: 978-1-907615-00-9

Printed in the UK by John Price Printers

This is more than just a book...

This is the start of a conversation about printmaking. By buying this book, you've joined that conversation, and we'd love to hear from you...

In this book you'll find photographic step-by-step instructions that will enable you to create your own range of stationery using lino printing, potato printing and stencilling. But unlike most books you buy, it doesn't stop there. Once you've had a go at printmaking yourself, you can upload and share photos of your creations, and any comments and ideas, onto our website at ↗ wwwhow2crafts.com. Then, once we've come to the end of the print run for this book, we'll select the best photos and comments and include them in the new edition of the book as a 'reader's appendix' – a source of inspiration and alternative designs for future readers.

As we've said on the how2crafts website, we believe crafts are all about conversation; the passing of skills and techniques from person to person down the ages. And we'd like our books to be part of that conversation. So it's only right that our books should change as the conversation progresses.

To join in the conversation visit
↗ **www.how2crafts.com/contribute**

Talk to us at
↗ **www.twitter.com/how2crafts**

Welcome to printmaking

This book is designed for the beginner print maker and is an excellent introduction to the art of printmaking. It is filled with ideas, information and a step-by-step guide on how to print using three different print processes for printing on to paper. We will be making a range of stationery products – greetings cards and envelopes, gift wrap, tags and labels and gift bags.

The three different print processes we will be using are:

- **Lino printing** is a block printing technique. You carve into a block to create a stamp, apply ink to the stamp and transfer the ink to the paper with pressure.

- **Potato printing** is probably the simplest printing method around. If you thought it was only for children, think again! It is a very easy yet effective method for printing onto paper.

- **Stencil printing** is what is known as a 'resist' method of printing, where the stencil is used to 'resist' or prevent the ink from reaching certain areas of the item to be printed, in order to create a design.

Inspiration

Before you start printing you need to know what you'll be printing! Where do artists get their inspiration from? I would say you can find inspiration pretty much everywhere you look.

My work has a strong emphasis on nature. I get most of my inspiration from my surroundings in and around Worcestershire in the UK – from flowers, plants, grasses and trees. I continually collect photographs, drawings and other visuals and these provide the inspiration for my work.

For other inspiration look at almost any aspect of art and design. I am influenced by traditional botanical drawings, Japanese art, the designs of the 1950's, artists' books, interior design, architecture and gardens.

Preparation

Printing is one of those crafts that can be done almost anywhere, but you will need a sturdy, flat surface – a surface with no holes or bumps. Your dining room table will almost certainly be fine.

Wear an apron and cover your work surface adequately – printing can be a very messy business. And make sure you have easy access to running water. This is essential for print making.

The inks we are using will dry by themselves without any help, but if you want them to dry quickly, a small electric fan heater or hair dryer is useful.

Have everything you need to hand before you start printing. Setting up can take a while but it will make printing much easier. I find being an organised printmaker helps!

And finally, make sure you have plenty of newspaper or scrap paper to hand – both for protecting surfaces and to practise printing on before printing on your chosen product.

Well now it's time to get started. Have fun and enjoy experimenting!

Lino printing
Equipment

You should be able to buy all the equipment and materials you'll need for lino printing from your local art and craft shop, or from numerous places online. You'll need the following items:

- **Printing inks**. I suggest using water-based printing inks as they are easy to clean. The inks usually come in quite basic colours, so experiment and try mixing your own.

- **Lino blocks**. You can buy lino in ready-cut blocks in a variety of sizes. Choose a size to match whatever you are printing on to.

- **A lino cutting set**. This normally consists of a wooden or plastic handle with a selection of interchangeable cutting tools.

- **Ink rollers**. It's worth getting a couple of ink rollers so you have one for inking and a clean one for applying pressure to the back of the lino block when you are printing.

- **Something to mix the inks with**. A spatula or old spoon will be suitable. In this book I've used a couple of wooden sticks.

- **A mixing/rolling palette**. A piece of perspex, or anything flat and non-porous will do. Make sure it's wide enough to take your roller.

- **Kitchen towel**. As I mentioned before, printing can be a very messy business!

- **A pencil and sketch pad**.

- **Tracing paper**.

- **Paper products to print onto**. For the lino printing I will be using standard A6 greetings cards and envelopes.

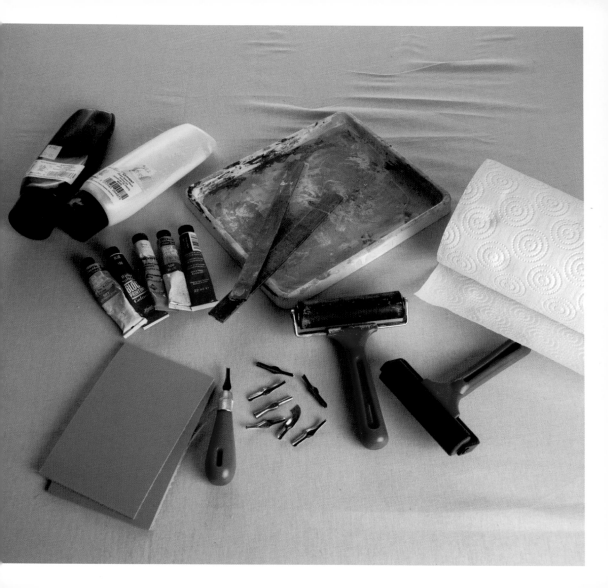

Sketching ideas and drawing your designs

After you've decided on a theme the next step is to sketch out your design. The print processes used in this book suit designs that are simple.

Once you have decided on a design to print, you'll need to draw the design out at the correct size so that it fits on to the material you will be printing on to.

You may already have a collection or sketchbook of drawings you want to use. If not, get sketching! Prepare the designs you want to try. In this book I am using a simple design based on seed heads, as shown on the right.

Tracing the design

With lino printing (and many other forms of printing), whatever design you cut into your lino block will be printed in reverse. You therefore need to transfer a mirror image of the design you have drawn onto the lino block. The easiest way to do this is to trace your drawing onto tracing paper (Fig 1) and then turn your tracing paper upside down and either draw directly over the drawing you can see through the tracing paper (Fig 2), or just heavily shade the back of the tracing paper with your pencil to transfer the design onto the lino block.

If the traced drawing on your lino block is a bit faint, go over it again with your pencil (Fig 3).

You're now ready to start carving your lino block (Fig 4).

Cutting the lino block

If this is your first foray into lino printing, experiment with your cutting tool on a spare piece of block. This will give you a feel for the technique required and will also give you a chance to work out what size cutting tool you are most comfortable with. I prefer the No. 2 cutter, but see what works best for you.

It might be obvious but it's worth pointing it out – the area you carve away will be the negative space, and the area of the block that is left (the raised area) will be what prints. Until you get used to lino printing it may help you to shade in with a pencil the areas you are going to remove. Because even though it might seem obvious, it can still be very easy to cut away the wrong bit of a drawing, and once you've done that there's no going back!

What you're aiming for is to cut away roughly half of the depth of the lino block in the areas where you don't want ink on your paper. Always carve away from you (Fig 5) as the cutters are very sharp. And try not to cut right through the block.

You'll find when you come to print your design that it's almost impossible to get a lino block to print completely 'clean', with no marks in the areas where you have cut the lino block away. Rather than seeing this as a failing however, you can cut your block in such a way as to make these incidental marks part of the design, adding to the quality of the print. With the design we are working with here, it might be nice to see some grasses at the bottom of the print, so cut in the direction you'd like to see grass at the bottom of the image (Fig 6).

Continue cutting until you have removed the lino in all the areas where you don't want ink on your paper (Figures 7 & 8).

Applying the ink

Now the fun bit! Once you are happy with your lino block, put a small amount of printing ink, roughly the size of a golf ball, onto your mixing surface and using your roller, spread the ink out evenly until the roller is completely covered with ink (Fig 9).

Place your lino block, cut side up, onto some newspaper or scrap paper to protect your work surface. Now apply the ink onto the lino block with the roller, until the raised area of the block is completely covered with ink (Fig 10).

I would recommend you do some test prints before printing your final products, so take some scrap paper and place the block face down onto the scrap paper (Fig 11).

To get an decent print you will need to apply even pressure to the lino block. You can use your hand, or better still a clean roller. Being careful not to let the lino move, roll repeatedly with some pressure over the back of the lino block with your roller (Fig 12).

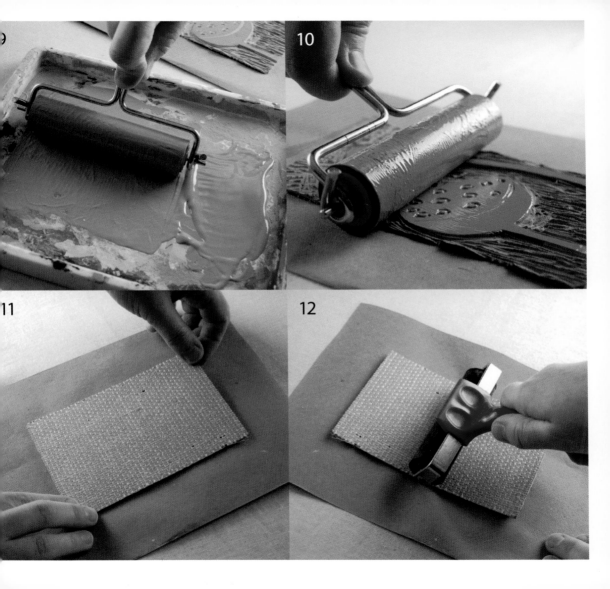

Making corrections

As you can see from my first test print (Fig 13), some of the lines haven't printed as well as I'd like. Don't panic if this happens – the good thing about lino printing is that you can go back and rework the lino block at any stage.

Clean off the ink with a paper towel (Fig 14) and decide which areas of the lino block you'd like to look at again. You may find you need to make some lines deeper or wider so they don't print, as I've had to do in Figure 15.

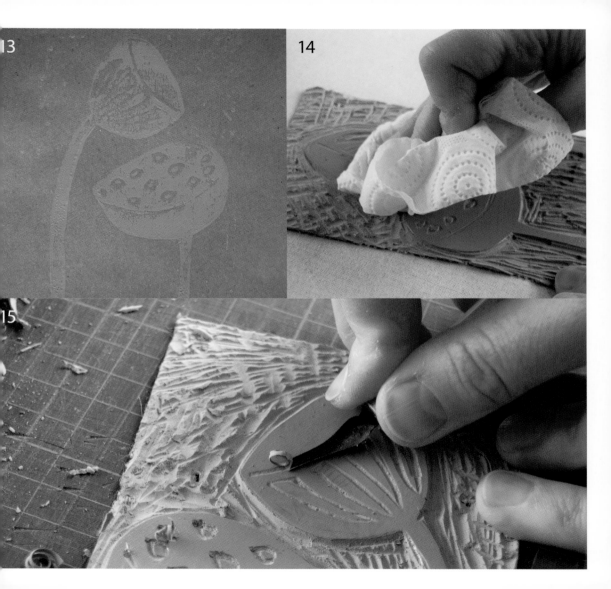

The final print

Now for the final print. Take your card and carefully place the lino block, inked side down, onto it (Fig 16) and roll as before with your clean roller (Fig 17).

Your finished card (Fig 18). As well as printing individual cards to send for an occasion, try creating a set of cards and envelopes, tie them together with a piece of ribbon and give them as a gift.

A lino block can be used over and over again, and as we're using water soluble inks, the lino block can be easily washed. Just rinse it under running water and dry it thoroughly.

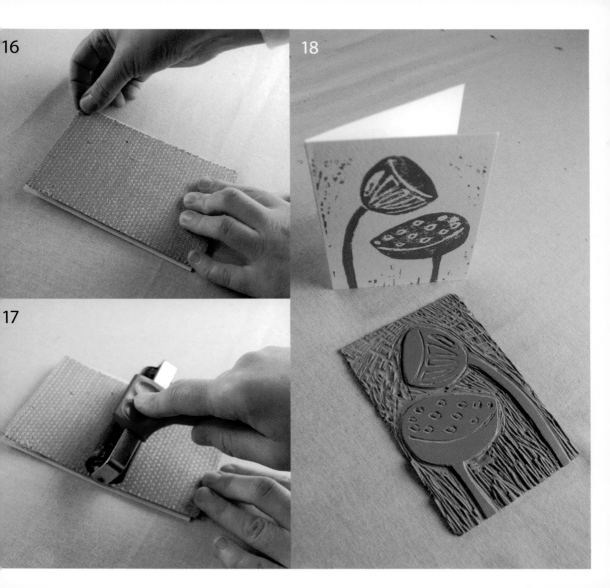

Potato printing
Equipment

Potato printing is a very simple form of printing that uses things most people will have round the home. You may think of it as an activity for children but with a good design and quality materials you'll get some great results, as I hope to show you here.

We're going to print some gift tags and wrapping paper to go with your lino-printed cards and the stencilled gift bags (see page 30).

You'll need the following:

- **Potatoes**. A good sized potato, nothing too small. Baking potatoes are fine.

- **A chopping board**

- **Kitchen roll**

- **Pencil and marker pen or felt pen**

- **Craft knife, sharp kitchen knife or a lino cutting set**

- **Printing inks**. You can use the same inks you used for lino printing (see page 8).

- **Something to mix the inks with**. A spatula or old spoon will be suitable. In this book I've used a couple of wooden sticks.

- **Paintbrushes or a sponge**

- **Paper products**. In this section we're printing on gift tags and wrapping paper.

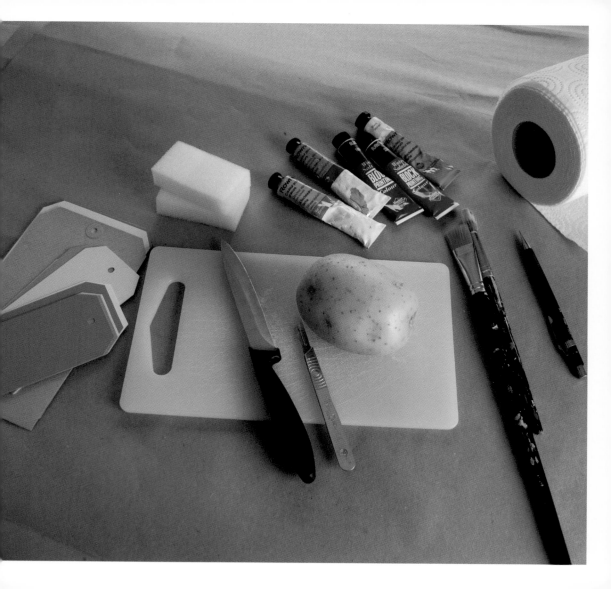

Cutting the potato

First of all you need to prepare your design. As with the lino printing you may want to sketch out a few thoughts before choosing your final design. I've gone for another natural design that will fit nicely with the seed head printed on my cards. The important thing to remember when creating your design is that simple shapes work best with potato printing.

Now cut your potato in half. Using kitchen towel, blot the potato to remove excess moisture from the surface.

Draw your design onto the potato. I find a felt pen works best (Fig 19).

Now using your knife or cutting tool (which ever you prefer – I use a kitchen knife) cut away the potato around the design until you are left with the design drawn on to a raised area of the potato (Fig 20). Then begin to cut away the areas of the design that you don't want to print. Don't be too worried about cutting accurately - potato printing is not a fine art!

Continue until your design is completely cut out (Fig 21).

Printing with the potato

Apply the ink to the potato using a paintbrush or a sponge. I find a sponge easier to use than a brush (Fig 22). Turn your potato over and press it evenly all over on to the paper (Fig 23). If you want to check how the print looks before printing on your tags or wrapping paper do a test run on a piece of scrap paper.

When ready to work on your final piece, press the potato firmly but evenly onto the surface. You'll probably need to re-ink the potato each time you print but depending on how much ink you have on the potato you may be able to get away with more than one print per inking (Fig 24). Experiment and see what works best.

If you want to print different colours you can re-use the same potato. Just wash the ink off under the tap and dry it off before applying the new colour. As it is a potato and not a lino block it won't last forever, so get as much use out of it on the day of use as possible.

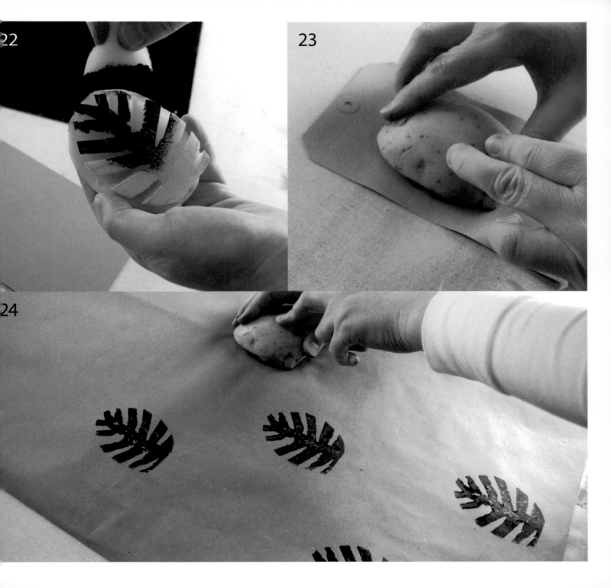

The finished article.

Now when you need to wrap a present, you can make it extra special by using your very own hand-printed gift wrap and tags. Add some ribbon, string or raffia for that special finishing touch.

Stencil printing
Equipment

Stencil printing is a simple method of transferring a pattern by brushing or sponging ink or paint through an open area of a cut stencil.

I'm going to be printing some gift bags.

You'll need the following:

- **Acetate**. For making the stencils.

- **Pencil and marker pen or felt pen**

- **Craft knife or scalpel**

- **Cutting mat**

- **Inks/paints**

- **Mixing palette**. I'm using an old plate.

- **Spatulas/stirring sticks/old spoons**

- **Cutting mat**

- **Masking tape**

- **Stencil brush or sponge**

- **Paper products**. I'm using gift bags.

Preparing the stencil

As with both the lino printing and the potato printing, a simple design works best with stencil printing. I've used a drawing of a berberis plant. Draw your design in your sketchbook and then trace it onto the acetate using your marker pen (Fig 25). Draw the design in the middle of your acetate, leaving room around it. This will protect the gift bag from any accidental marks while printing.

Now start to cut out your design with your knife (Fig 26). While acetate makes very good stencils, it can be tricky to cut and it's very easy to slip with your knife. You may want to practise cutting a sheet before cutting out your actual stencil.

If you're printing different colours as we are doing, you'll need to cut a stencil for each colour you want to use (Fig 27). This will stop colours from mixing and getting in unwanted areas.

When you've cut out all three stencils, place the first stencil onto the bag in the place where you want the stencil to appear. Use small pieces of masking tape to fix it firmly in place so it can't move during the printing process (Fig 28).

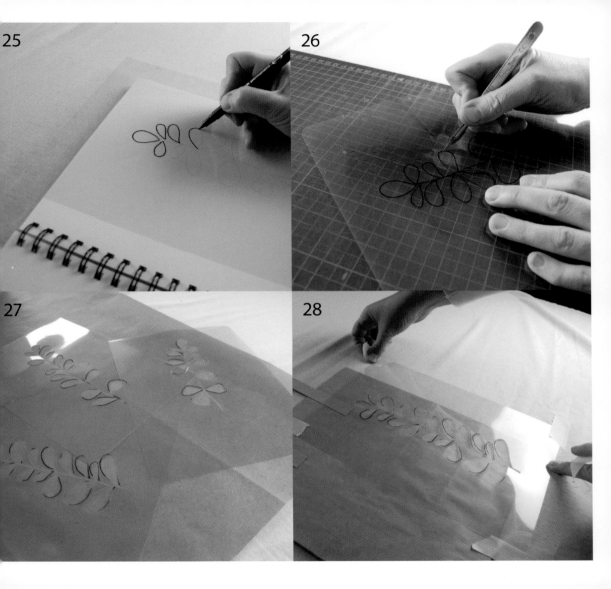

Printing

Put a small amount of ink of your chosen colour onto your palette or plate. Apply some ink to your brush or sponge and begin to gently dab the ink through the stencil (Fig 29). Apply several thin layers of ink until the area is evenly covered.

If you are printing more than one colour, let the first colour dry before printing the next and use a different sponge or brush for each colour (Fig 30).

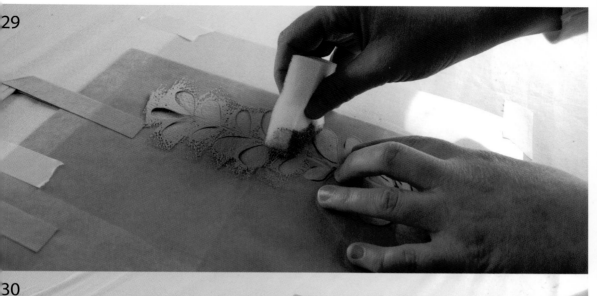

You now have a beautifully stencilled bag. Add one of your printed gift tags to finish it off.

Remember you can print on almost anything, so experiment with different papers, different inks and play around with colour. I'm sure you will come up with some great combinations. And when you do, don't forget to upload your pictures on to the how2crafts website, to be in with a chance of getting yourself in print. Visit ↗ **www.how2crafts.com/contribute**

Suppliers

United Kingdom
There are many online suppliers of printing equipment and materials. One I'd recommend for general art and craft supplies is:
↗ **www.greatart.co.uk**

For greetings cards blanks and envelopes try:
↗ **www.craftcreations.com**

For suppliers in other countries, Google 'craft supplies' and 'blank cards'.

About the author

Sarah Roberts began her career studying painting but later went on to study textiles and surface pattern at Batley School of Art & Design in West Yorkshire, UK. This is where her love of printmaking started. Whilst at college Sarah received an RSA Design Award.

Sarah has been working as a self-employed artist for almost 10 years. She has been featured in magazines such as Country Living and Country Homes & Interiors and has exhibited at contemporary craft shows such as the contemporary Craft Fair in Bovey Tracey and at Origin in London. Sarah also sells work through art and craft galleries throughout the UK.